IDAHO

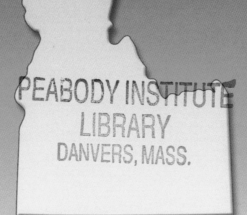

by Jonatha A. Brown

GARETHSTEVENS
GS
PUBLISHING
A Member of the WRC Media Family of Companies

Please visit our web site at: www.garethstevens.com
For a free color catalog describing Gareth Stevens Publishing's
list of high-quality books and multimedia programs, call
1-800-542-2595 (USA) or 1-800-387-3178 (Canada).
Gareth Stevens Publishing's fax: (414) 332-3567.

Library of Congress Cataloging-in-Publication Data

Brown, Jonatha A.
    Idaho / Jonatha A. Brown.
        p. cm. — (Portraits of the states)
    Includes bibliographical references and index.
    ISBN-10: 0-8368-4700-8 — ISBN-13: 978-0-8368-4700-0 (lib. bdg.)
    ISBN-10: 0-8368-4717-2 — ISBN-13: 978-0-8368-4717-8 (softcover)
    1. Idaho—Juvenile literature. I. Title. II. Series.
    F746.3.B75   2007
    979.6—dc22   2005036635

This edition first published in 2007 by
Gareth Stevens Publishing
A Member of the WRC Media Family of Companies
330 West Olive Street, Suite 100
Milwaukee, WI 53212 USA

This edition copyright © 2007 by Gareth Stevens, Inc.

Editorial direction: Mark J. Sachner
Project manager: Jonatha A. Brown
Editor: Catherine Gardner
Art direction and design: Tammy West
Picture research: Diane Laska-Swanke
Indexer: Walter Kronenberg
Production: Jessica Morris and Robert Kraus

Picture credits: Cover, pp. 15, 24 © John Elk III; pp. 4, 22 © Glenn Oakley/
Idaho Stock Images; pp. 5, 17, 29 © Steve Bly/Idaho Stock Images; pp. 6, 21
© Leland Howard/Idaho Stock Images; p. 8 © Hulton Archive/Getty Images; p. 9
© MPI/Getty Images; pp. 11, 12 © Bettmann/CORBIS; p. 16 © Marc Auth/Idaho
Stock Images; p. 18 © Kirk Anderson/Idaho Stock Images; p. 25 © AP Images;
p. 26 © Milan Chuckovich/Idaho Stock Images; p. 27 © Marjorie McBride/Idaho
Stock Images; p. 28 © Aflo Photo/Allsport/Getty Images

Printed in the United States of America

1 2 3 4 5 6 7 8 9 10 09 08 07 06

CONTENTS

★ ★

Chapter 1 Introduction 4

Chapter 2 History 6

Time Line 13

Chapter 3 People 14

Chapter 4 The Land 18

Chapter 5 Economy 22

Chapter 6 Government 24

Chapter 7 Things to See and Do 26

Glossary 30

To Find Out More 31

Index 32

Words that are defined in the Glossary appear
in **bold** the first time they are used in the text.

On the Cover: Idaho is full of natural beauty. Here, the Sawtooth
Mountains tower over Redfish Lake.

Introduction

What would you like to do in Idaho? Paddle a canoe on a clear mountain lake? Watch elk drink at the water's edge? Perhaps you would like to follow the trail of early explorers or ski down some of the best slopes in the United States? You can do all these things and more in Idaho.

Idaho is in the Rocky Mountains. It has high peaks, sparkling rivers, and peaceful lakes. Yet the land is not all wilderness. Farmers grow potatoes and wheat. Factories make computer parts and other goods. Museums and historical sites show how Natives and settlers lived here long ago.

The people of Idaho are proud of their beautiful state. They hope you will like it, too.

A skier glides over the snow at a resort in Coeur d'Alene.

The state flag of Idaho.

IDAHO FACTS

- Became the 43rd U.S. State: July 3, 1890
- Population (2004): 1,393,262
- Capital: Boise
- Biggest Cities: Boise, Nampa, Pocatello, Idaho Falls
- Size: 82,747 square miles (214,315 square kilometers)
- Nickname: The Gem State
- State Tree: Western white pine
- State Flower: White syringa, or mock orange
- State Horse: Appaloosa
- State Bird: Mountain bluebird

History

Native Americans have lived in Idaho for thousands of years. The earliest people hunted animals and gathered wild plants to eat. Over the years, the Natives developed two main ways of life. The northern tribes lived in the mountains, near the rivers. They caught fish and hunted deer and other big game. The southern tribes lived on the prairies. They ate seeds, bird eggs, and cactuses. They hunted birds and small animals, too. Some fished for salmon.

Long ago, Native Americans lived near Lake Pend Oreille.

White Explorers

White men reached the area for the first time in 1805. They came from the East Coast of the United States. The leaders of the group were Meriwether Lewis and William Clark. They wrote about the wonderful places they saw on their trip. Soon, more explorers arrived. American and British trappers came, too. They trapped animals for their fur.

In 1809, a Canadian man named David Thompson set up a fur trading post at Lake Pend Oreille. He called it Kullyspell House. It was the first white settlement in Idaho. By the 1830s, other trading posts had been built along the rivers.

Some white people came to Idaho to spread religion. They were **missionaries**. These people wanted to teach the Natives about their God. Henry Spalding was an early missionary. He set up a church in Lapwai in 1836.

A Growing Area

At that time, both the United States and Britain wanted to take control of the land in the Pacific Northwest. They agreed to split this huge area in 1846. Britain kept the land in western Canada.

The United States kept the land that is now Idaho, Washington, and Oregon.

Gold was found at Orofino Creek and Grimes Creek in the early 1860s. Thousands of people rushed to these areas, hoping to get rich. Idaho City became a big mining center. For a short time, it was the largest city in the Northwest.

FUN FACTS

A First for Franklin

In the mid-1800s, a group of Christians moved north from Utah. These people were **Mormons**. They built the town of Franklin in 1860. It was the first long-lasting white town in Idaho.

The Idaho **Territory** was formed in 1863. It grew quickly. Silver and lead were discovered in the 1880s, and this drew even more miners to the area. Over time, some of these men stopped mining and began farm-ing. At the same time, roads and railroads were being built. This made travel easier.

Thousands of settlers came to Idaho in the 1800s. Most of them traveled in covered wagons. The wagons were pulled by horses, mules, and oxen.

Fights for the Land

During the 1850s, the U.S. government signed **treaties** with Native tribes in Idaho. The tribes gave up most of their land and got very little in return. They were sent to live on **reservations**.

Many Natives grew angry about the way they were treated. Problems between whites and Natives grew. Sometimes, one group attacked the other. The fighting continued for years. In the end, the whites were stronger. By 1880, all of the Native tribes had been defeated.

Chief Joseph's real name was Inmutooyahlatlat. This means "Thunder Rolling Down the Mountain." He tried to keep peace between his people and the whites. Both whites and Natives respected him.

IN IDAHO'S HISTORY

An Escape that Failed

In 1877, a group of Nez Percé left their reservation in Idaho. Led by Chief Joseph, they tried to escape to Canada. The U.S. Army chased them, and the two groups fought for months. Finally, the Natives were caught. When Chief Joseph gave up, he said these famous words: "Hear me, my chiefs! I am tired. My heart is sick and sad. From where the sun now stands I will fight no more forever."

A New State

More white people moved to Idaho over the next few years. Many became sheep and cattle ranchers. Others built roads and railroads. As travel grew easier, even more people moved here. Idaho became a U.S. state in 1890.

The new state had good soil, but it did not receive much rain. The land was too dry for most crops. In the early 1900s, **irrigation** systems were built. They brought water from the rivers to the fields. Now, farmers in Idaho could grow more crops.

In 1915, the Arrowrock Dam was built across the Boise River. The lake that formed behind it provided water for more farmland.

Famous People of Idaho

Gutzon Borglum

Born: March 25, 1867, Ovid, Idaho

Died: March 6, 1941, Chicago, Illinois

Gutzon Borglum was born in a log cabin. He studied art and became a great **sculptor**. In the 1920s, he started carving a huge **memorial** to the United States. It became the Mount Rushmore National Memorial. This memorial was carved out of a huge cliff. It features the heads of four U.S. presidents. They are George Washington, Thomas Jefferson, Abraham Lincoln, and Theodore Roosevelt. Each head is 60 feet (18.3 meters) high! Thousands of people visit the Black Hills of South Dakota each year to see this famous work of art.

IN IDAHO'S HISTORY

Problems in the Mines

In 1892, the price of silver fell. Mine owners paid their workers less and closed some of the mines. This made the miners angry. When the miners blew up a mine near Wallace, soldiers were called in to **restore** peace. Some miners were sent to jail. This did not end the problems between mine owners and workers. In 1899, miners blew up another mine. Once again, soldiers were called in to restore calm.

Mining brought lots of money into Idaho in the late 1800s and early 1900s. Some mine owners grew very rich.

Farming became the biggest business in the state.

Forestry grew at the same time. Trees were cut down and shipped to lumber mills. There, the trees were made into lumber for building.

Wars Bring Change

The United States fought in two world wars in the first half of the 1900s. Many people from Idaho became soldiers. Farmers grew food for the troops. Workers in factories built airplane parts and guns needed for the war.

After World War II, more dams were built. Lakes formed behind the dams. The lake water was used to make electric power for homes and factories.

This school was in a prison camp for Japanese Americans in Twin Falls. Many children lived there during World War II.

IN IDAHO'S HISTORY

A Bad Mistake

The United States fought Japan in World War II. During the war, the U.S. government treated Japanese Americans badly. It made many of them leave their homes along the Pacific Coast and move to prison camps. One of these camps was built in Twin Falls. During the war, it housed ten thousand Japanese Americans. They were forced to live there even though they had done nothing wrong. This was very unfair. Years later, the U.S. government said it was sorry.

In 1951, a power plant near Arco made electricity in a new way. It used nuclear energy. Arco became the first city in the world to get all of its electric power from a nuclear power plant.

Idaho Today

In the 1970s, the people of Idaho took steps to protect the natural beauty of their state. They passed laws to save rivers, streams, and wild places. Land was set aside for national forests, too. Today, people come from near and far to enjoy this beautiful state.

about 1700	Native Americans in what is now Idaho begin breeding and taming horses.
1805	Lewis and Clark reach present-day Idaho.
1809	A fur trader builds Kullyspell, the first white trading post in the area.
1860	Gold is discovered at Orofino Creek.
1863	The Idaho Territory is set up.
1877	Chief Joseph and the Nez Percé are beaten by the U.S. Army.
1880s	Silver and lead are found in Idaho.
1890	Idaho becomes a U.S. state on July 3.
1899	Miners blow up a mining operation because they are paid so poorly.
1915	The Arrowrock Dam is completed on the Boise River.
1917–1918	The United States enters World War I. People from Idaho fight in the war and grow food for soldiers.
1941–1945	People from Idaho join the war effort as the United States fights in World War II.
1942	10,000 Japanese Americans are are forced to live in a camp in Idaho until World War II ends.
1976	Hells Canyon National Recreation Area is created along the Snake River.

People

Idaho is a large state, but it does not have a large **population**. Fewer than 1.5 million people live here. In recent years, more and more people have found that this state is a great place to live and work. Today, Idaho is growing much faster than most other states.

Boise is a city in the western part of the state. It is the biggest city in Idaho. About one-third of the people in the state live in or near Boise. Coeur d'Alene is the largest city in the **panhandle**. Pocatello

Hispanics

This chart shows the different racial backgrounds of people in Idaho. In the 2000 U.S. Census, 7.9 percent of the people in Idaho called themselves Latino or Hispanic. Most of them or their relatives came from places where Spanish is spoken. Hispanics do not appear on this chart because they may come from any racial background.

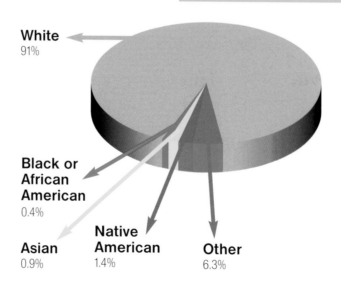

The People of Idaho

Total Population 1,393,262

White
91%

Black or African American
0.4%

Asian
0.9%

Native American
1.4%

Other
6.3%

Percentages are based on the 2000 Census.

and Idaho Falls are the biggest cities in the east.

About four in every ten people in Idaho live in the country. This makes Idaho more **rural** than most U.S. states. Even so, most people who are new to the state move to the cities and big towns. Between 1990 and 2000, Boise grew by almost 50 percent. Some of the smaller cities in the state grew even faster.

People from Near and Far

Thousands of non-Native people moved to Idaho in the late 1800s. Some came from the eastern United States, Canada, Britain, and Germany. Others came from Asia. Thousands of Chinese worked in the mines. Many Japanese came to the state, too. They helped build the early railroads.

Young girls perform a folk dance at a Basque festival in Idaho. Their bright red dresses and lively steps have attracted quite a crowd.

Large numbers of **Basques** also came. They were from the Pyrenees Mountains in Spain and France. They had been sheepherders there. They were sheepherders in Idaho, too. Today, more Basques live here than in any other state in the country.

People are still coming to Idaho from other countries. Many move to this state from Mexico. Others come from China and Vietnam. Most people who move here, however, come from other U.S. states.

Religion

Many people who live in Idaho are Mormons. They are Christians who are members of the Church of

Jesus Christ of Latter-day Saints. Other people who live in the state are Roman Catholics, Baptists, and Methodists. Jews, Hindus, and Buddhists live here, too.

Education

Henry Spalding set up the first school in Idaho in 1837. It was a missionary school for Native boys and girls. More than twenty years later, Mormons opened the first school for white children. This school was in Franklin.

The University of Idaho in Moscow was founded in 1889. It is the oldest university in the state. Today, Idaho is home to more than one dozen colleges and universities. The largest of them is Boise State College.

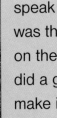

Famous People of Idaho

Sacagawea

Born: about 1786, near Salmon, Idaho

Died: unknown

Sacagawea was a Native American of the Shoshone tribe. She was captured by another tribe while she was a girl. Later, she married a French trader. In 1804, Lewis and Clark hired her and her husband to help them explore the land in the West. Sacagawea was very helpful. She found trails through the wilderness. When the men needed fresh food, she found wild plants to eat. When they met Natives along the way, she helped them speak together. She was the only woman on the trip, and she did a great deal to make it a success.

The Land

Idaho is in the northwestern United States. The state has an odd shape. It is much narrower in the north than in the south. The narrow part in the north is called the panhandle.

The Rocky Mountains

Mountain ranges cover more than one-half of the state. Most of these ranges are in the Rocky Mountains. One range in "the Rockies" is the Bitterroot Range. It runs along Idaho's border with Montana. The Sawtooth Range lies farther west. This range has high, jagged peaks that look like the teeth of a saw. More mountains are found near the border between Idaho and Wyoming.

FUN FACTS

Miles and Miles of Rivers

Idaho has more miles of rivers than any other U.S. state. In total, the state has 3,100 miles (4,989 km) of rivers! They are home to bass, perch, and trout. Geese, ducks, eagles, herons, otters, and mink can also be found.

Borah Peak stands tall in the Lost River Range. It is the highest peak in the state.

IDAHO

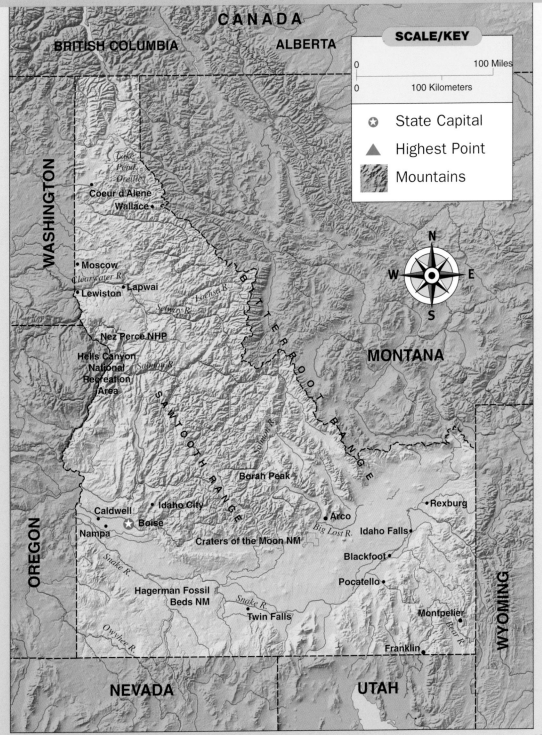

SCALE/KEY

0   100 Miles

0   100 Kilometers

✪ State Capital

▲ Highest Point

Mountains

CANADA

BRITISH COLUMBIA   ALBERTA

WASHINGTON

Lake Pend Oreille
• Coeur d'Alene
Wallace •

• Moscow
Clearwater R.
• Lewiston   • Lapwai
Lochsa R.
Selway R.

BITTERROOT RANGE

MONTANA

• Nez Perce NHP

Hells Canyon
National
Recreation
Area
Salmon R.

SAWTOOTH RANGE

Salmon R.

Borah Peak

• Idaho City
Caldwell •
• Boise ✪
Nampa •

Arco •
Big Lost R.
Idaho Falls •

• Rexburg

Craters of the Moon NM

Blackfoot •

Snake R.

Pocatello •

Hagerman Fossil
Beds NM
Snake R.
• Twin Falls

Montpelier •
Bear R.

Franklin •

OREGON

NEVADA   UTAH

WYOMING

Owyhee R.

The highest point in the state is Borah Peak. It is 12,662 feet (3,859 m) high. This peak is in the Lost River Range.

The Rocky Mountains are rugged and beautiful. Hundreds of clear blue lakes lie between the high peaks. Sparkling rivers run from some of these lakes to other parts of the state. In some places, rivers have carved deep canyons in the earth.

Deep green forests of pine and fir grow in this area. The western white pine is very common. It is the state tree. Grassy meadows can also be found. Each year in the spring, wildflowers fill the meadows with color. Deer, elk, mountain goats, bighorn sheep, and moose roam here. Bobcats, bear, and coyotes prowl along the edges of the meadows and among the trees.

Major Rivers

Snake River
1,038 miles (1,670 km) long

Salmon River
420 miles (676 km) long

Clearwater River
185 miles (298 km) long

Snow often falls in the mountains. The high peaks are much colder than the valleys and canyons.

The Columbia Plateau

Flatter land makes up the Columbia **Plateau**. Most of the plateau lies near the Snake River. It is up to 50 miles (80 km) wide in some places. The land is good for farming. The climate is milder than it is in the mountains, but little rain and snow fall. Most of the farmland is irrigated.

A smaller part of the plateau lies near Idaho's

border with Washington and Oregon. This area has small mountains and gently rolling hills. It is home to Hells Canyon, the most famous **gorge** in the state. The soil is good for farming, and the climate in this area is mild and wetter than it is along the Snake River.

The Great Basin

The Great Basin lies in the southeastern corner of Idaho. Hills and mountains dot the land. Big stretches of sand and gravel lie between them. This area gets little rain, and it is colder than the plateau. In some places, sagebrush and

FUN FACTS

Super Deep!

Some people think the deepest gorge in North America is the Grand Canyon. This is not true. Hells Canyon is deeper. It was created over thousands of years by the waters of the Snake River. Hells Canyon is about 7,900 feet (2,407 m) deep. It is about 2,000 feet (610 m) deeper than the Grand Canyon!

grasses grow. Pronghorn and coyotes live here. Rabbits and other small animals live here, too.

The Snake River winds through Hells Canyon. The canyon lies on the border between Idaho and Oregon.

Economy

Long ago, most of the settlers in Idaho worked on farms, in mines, and in the forests. Much has changed since then. These days, more people work in offices and factories.

Big machines harvest potatoes in an Idaho field.

Making Goods

Manufacturing has been the top industry in the state since the 1970s. Many of the factories make high-tech products, such as computer parts and printers. Others make processed foods from the crops and farm animals raised in the state. They make frozen and dried potato products, flour, cheese, meat, and much more. Wood and paper products are also made from trees cut in the state's forests.

Helping Tourists

In recent years, tourism has created many jobs in Idaho. Tourists stay in hotels. They eat in restaurants. They go to ski resorts and buy lift tickets. All of these places need many workers to help the tourists.

Farming

Farming still provides jobs for many people. Idaho produces more potatoes than any other state. Peas, dried beans, wheat, and barley are also important. Cattle and sheep are raised here, too.

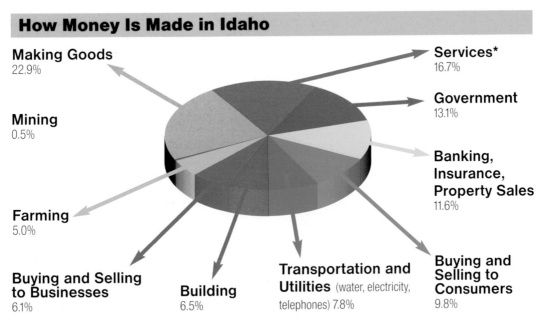

How Money Is Made in Idaho

Making Goods
22.9%

Services*
16.7%

Government
13.1%

Mining
0.5%

Banking,
Insurance,
Property Sales
11.6%

Farming
5.0%

Buying and Selling
to Businesses
6.1%

Building
6.5%

Transportation and
Utilities (water, electricity,
telephones) 7.8%

Buying and
Selling to
Consumers
9.8%

* Services include jobs in hotels, restaurants, auto repair, medicine, teaching, and entertainment.

Government

Boise is the capital of Idaho. The state's leaders work there. The government of the state has three parts. They are the executive, legislative, and judicial branches.

Executive Branch

The executive branch carries out the state's laws. The governor is the head of this branch. The lieutenant governor helps the governor. Other officials also work in this branch.

The state capitol building is in Boise. It looks much like the U.S. Capitol in Washington, D.C.

Legislative Branch

The legislative branch has two parts. They are the Senate and the House of Representatives. These two groups work together to make laws for the state.

The state legislature meets in Boise. It meets for about ninety days each year.

Judicial Branch

Judges and courts make up the judicial branch. The judges and courts may decide whether people who have been accused of committing crimes are guilty.

Local Governments

Forty-four counties are in the state. Each county is run by three people known as commissioners. Many towns and cities are led by a mayor and council.

IDAHO'S STATE GOVERNMENT

Executive		Legislative		Judicial	
Office	**Length of Term**	**Body**	**Length of Term**	**Court**	**Length of Term**
Governor	4 years	Senate (35 members)	2 years	Supreme (5 justices)	6 years
Lieutenant Governor	4 years	House of Representatives (70 members)	2 years	Appeals (3 judges)	6 years

Things to See and Do

If you like to explore wild places, you will love Idaho! The Frank Church—River of No Return Wilderness is one of the largest wilderness areas in the nation. You can backpack, camp, pack in on horses, or go by raft or canoe. Hike on trails if you like, or find your own way. In this rugged land of mountains and rivers, you may see bear, deer, and elk. You can fish in the sparkling streams and catch trout for your dinner. In the quiet

A fisherman casts a fly on the quiet waters of Little Redfish Lake.

evenings, you can enjoy a campfire under the stars.

The Hells Canyon National Recreation Area is special, too. There, you can camp, fish, and ride rafts down the Snake River. You can also hike in the mountains and find traces of the Native tribes who lived here long ago. The state also has many national forests and parks.

The Salmon River is famous for it rapids. These

The mighty Salmon River offers lots of excitement. Here, guests gasp as a guide steers their raft through a stretch of rapids.

Famous People of Idaho

Frank Church

Born: July 25, 1924, Boise, Idaho

Died: April 7, 1984, Bethesda, Maryland

Frank Church was born and raised in Idaho. As a young man, he became a great public speaker. Later, he represented his state in the U.S. Senate. He served from 1957 to 1981. In the Senate, he helped the United States work with other countries around the world. He also helped lead the fight to protect the environment. The Frank Church—River of No Return Wilderness was named after him not long before he died.

churning waters can provide quite a roller coaster ride. Going downstream on this river is hard. Going back up is much harder. For this reason, the Salmon is known as the River of No Return. It is one of the top whitewater rivers in the world.

The Past Comes Alive

The people of Idaho are proud of their past. In the town of Wallace, you can see how miners lived long ago. Near Lapwai, you can learn

Famous People of Idaho

Picabo Street

Born: April 3, 1971, Triumph, Idaho

Picabo (peek-a-boo) Street was named after a village in Idaho. As a child, she helped out on her family's farm. She played football with boys who lived nearby and learned to ski, too. She became such a good skier that she became the National Junior Alpine Ski Champion. In 1994, she won a silver medal at the Olympics. Four years later, she won a gold medal. Picabo Street has inspired many girls who love to play sports.

Picabo Street races down a steep slope during the 1998 Winter Olympics. She wins the Super G and takes home a gold medal!

The streets of Wallace still look much as they did in the late 1800s. Back then, Wallace was a busy mining town. Today, you can visit Wallace to see how silver miners once lived and worked.

about the Nez Percé and their history. This area has many historical sites. You can drive along Highway 12 near the Lochsa River. This road follows the trail taken long ago by the explorers Lewis and Clark.

The famous Oregon Trail once passed through Idaho. Thousands of settlers walked and rode along this trail as they made their way west. Today, you can spend time at a museum in Montpelier to learn about life on the trail in the 1800s.

GLOSSARY

★ ★

Basques — people who came from the Pyrenees Mountains in Spain and France

gorge — canyon

irrigation — bringing water to fields through pipes and canals

manufacturing — making goods in factories

memorial — something that honors an important person, event, or thing

missionaries — people who go to another land to spread religion

Mormons — members of a Christian church known as the Church of Jesus Christ of Latter-day Saints

panhandle — a narrow area of land that juts out from the rest of the state

plateau — a large, flat area that is higher than the land around it

population — the number of people who live in a place such as a city, town, or state

reservations — areas of land set apart by the government for a special purpose

restore — bring back

rural — having to do with the countryside or life in the country

sculptor — a person who carves figures in wood, clay, or stone

territory — an area of land that belongs to a country

treaties — written agreements

Books

A Picture Book of Sacagawea. Picture Book Biography (series). David A. Adler (Holiday House)

Chief Joseph of the Nez Perce. Photo-Illustrated Biographies (series). Bill McAuliffe (Capstone Press)

Idaho. Rookie Read-About Geography (series). Pam Zollman (Children's Press)

Life on the Oregon Trail. Picture the Past (series). Sally Senzell Isaacs (Heinemann)

P Is for Potato: An Idaho Alphabet. Discover America State By State (series). Stan and Joy Steiner (Sleeping Bear Press)

Web Sites

Enchanted Learning: Idaho
www.enchantedlearning.com/usa/states/idaho/

Go West Across America with Lewis and Clark
www.nationalgeographic.com/features/97/west/

Idaho Forest Products Commission: Forests Are for Kids!
www.idahoforests.org/kids1.htm

Idaho: Just for Kids
www.accessidaho.org/education/kids.html

INDEX

African Americans 14
Appaloosa ponies 7
Arco 12
Arrowrock Dam 10
Asian Americans 12, 14, 15

Basques 16
Bitterroot Range 18
Boise 5, 14, 15, 24, 25, 27
Boise River 10
Boise State College 17
Borah Peak 18, 20
Borglum, Gutzon 10

Canada 7, 9, 15
China 15, 16
Church, Frank 27
Clark, William 6, 17, 29
Clearwater River 20
Coeur d'Alene 4, 14
Columbia Plateau 20–21
counties 25
covered wagons 8

education 17

France 16
Franklin 8, 17

gold 8
Great Basin 21
Great Britain 7, 15

Grimes Creek 8

Hells Canyon 21, 27
Hispanics 14

Idaho City 8
Idaho Falls 15
Idaho Territory 8

Japan 12, 15
Joseph, Chief 9

Lake Pend Oreille 7
Lapwai 7, 28
lead 8, 13
Lewis, Meriwether 6, 17, 29
Little Redfish Lake 26
Lochsa River 29
Lost River Range 18, 20

Mexico 16
mining 8, 11, 23, 29
missionaries 7, 17
Montpelier 29
Mormons 8, 16–17

Native Americans 6, 7, 9, 14, 17, 27, 29
Nez Percé people 7, 9, 29

Oregon Trail 7, 29
Orofino Creek 8
Ovid 10

panhandle 14, 18

Pocatello 14
potatoes 22, 23

railroads 8, 15
religion 16–17
reservations 9
rivers 18, 20
Rocky Mountains 15, 18, 20

Sacagawea 17
Salmon 17
Salmon River 20, 27–28
Sawtooth Range 18, 26
Shoshone people 17
silver 8, 11, 13, 29
skiing 4, 26, 28
Snake River 20, 21, 27
Spain 7, 16
Spalding, Henry 7, 17
Street, Picabo 28
Sun Valley 26

Thompson, David 7
tourism 23
Twin Falls 12

University of Idaho 17

Vietnam 16

Wallace 11, 28, 29
World War I 13
World War II 11, 12